P9-CSA-637
987370

987370

P9-CSA-637

BIG DIGS

AND CONSTRUCTION SITES

JOHN DEERE

BIG DIGS
AND CONSTRUCTION SITES

By Pat Fortunato-Chisena

Spring Valley Public Library
121 West Jefferson St.
Spring Valley, MN 55975

DK Publishing

PARACHUTE PRESS

JOHN DEERE
LICENSED PRODUCT

LONDON, NEW YORK, MUNICH,
MELBOURNE, and DELHI

Editor Nancy Ellwood
Assistant Editor Liza Kaplan
Designer Jessica Park
Managing Art Editor Michelle Baxter
Publishing Director Beth Sutinis

Book Designer Greg Wozney
Associate Designer Annemarie Redmond

Special thanks to David Althaus
and Michael H. Porter

Copyright © 2009 Deere & Company.

Published in the United States by
DK Publishing
375 Hudson Street
New York, New York 10014

09 10 11 12 13 10 9 8 7 6 5 4 3 2 1

Created and produced by
Parachute Publishing, L.L.C.
322 Eighth Avenue
New York, NY 10001

All rights reserved. No part of this publication may be
reproduced, stored in a retrieval system, or transmitted in
any form or by any means, electronic, mechanical,
photocopying, recording, or otherwise, without the prior
written permission of the copyright owner.

A catalog record for this book is
available from the Library of Congress.

ISBN 978-0-7566-4448-2

Printed in Malaysia by Imago
June 2009, first printing.

Discover more at
www.dk.com

Contents

The construction site

The **construction site** is a busy place, filled with big machines doing big jobs. Here you'll find machines that clear ground, dig holes, and put up buildings. Buildings can be big or small, high or low. No matter what their size, all buildings begin on a construction site.

Powerful machines like this **excavator** are found on construction sites. An excavator digs big holes.

Workers have many different kinds of jobs on a construction site. This man is a **machine operator**. He runs the excavator.

What we build

All around the world, every day of every week, something is being built—from small houses to tall buildings to large amusement parks. How many kinds of buildings can you think of? Here are some.

Many people live in apartment buildings, especially in cities.

Sport fans go to stadiums to see their favorite teams play.

A school can be as small as one room or as big as this one.

After a product is made in a factory . . .

One day you might work in an office building like this.

. . . it is sold in stores and shopping malls.

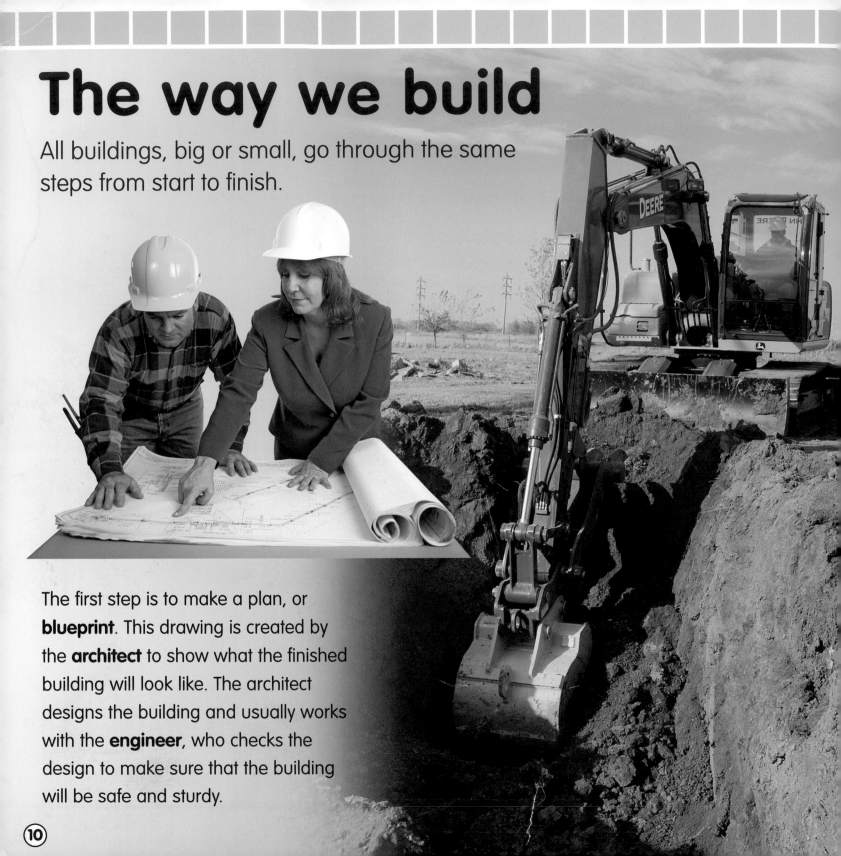

The way we build

All buildings, big or small, go through the same steps from start to finish.

The first step is to make a plan, or **blueprint**. This drawing is created by the **architect** to show what the finished building will look like. The architect designs the building and usually works with the **engineer**, who checks the design to make sure that the building will be safe and sturdy.

Once the blueprint is approved, the site has to be cleared. That's where bulldozers and other big machines come in.

An excavator digs a huge hole for the **foundation**, which will support the building and keep it strong.

Next, the **framework** is built. The framework is the structure that supports the building. It's usually made of wood for houses, and steel for larger buildings.

After that, a plumber puts in pipes that will carry water and waste.

Walls are built next. Some walls use concrete blocks; others use panels made from plaster, called **drywall**. Once the walls are in place, they are painted.

The new building needs lights, sinks, toilets, bathtubs, and more.

When the building is finished, trees, plants, and lawns are planted around it. This is called **landscaping**.

Big machines

Here are five machines that may be found on a construction site.

A **bulldozer** pushes dirt, sand, and **rubble** to clear the ground. Rubble is made up of broken pieces of stone and brick. It often comes from a building that was torn down.

A **dump truck** has a back gate that opens to dump out soil, stones, and other material.

A **loader** has a wide, square bucket that tilts. The loader lifts and moves heavy loads.

A **backhoe** has a loader bucket on the front and a digging bucket on the back. It can do two jobs: digging and lifting.

Did You Know?

Big machines are also called **heavy equipment**. They can weigh anywhere from 2 tons to more than 90 tons.

An **excavator** has a long arm that digs, lifts, and moves material. It can dig a hole as deep as 45 feet (13.5 m).

The bulldozer

One of the first machines you'll find at work on a construction site is a bulldozer. This tough machine works hard to clear the ground and make it level so building can begin.

A bulldozer has a powerful **engine** that powers the machine so it can do a lot of heavy work.

FUN FACT

Some people think that this machine is called a bulldozer because it sounds like a bull. Others say it got its name because it's so strong and can push with the power of many, many bulls.

A bulldozer has a wide metal **blade** on the front. This pushes soil, sand, tree trunks, rocks, and rubble out of the way to make the ground level.

The **cab** is where the operator sits to operate the machine.

Hard worker

Most construction jobs begin with clearing the land. That's a bulldozer's most important job.

Thick **crawler tracks** keep the bulldozer steady, so it can go over big bumps and holes. They also help keep the dozer from sinking into sandy ground or getting stuck in the mud.

The bulldozer at work

A bulldozer does many jobs on a construction site. Besides pushing soil and clearing ground, it can pull and move heavy things.

Ripping up

Bulldozers use an attachment called a **ripper** to tear through very hard ground. After the ripper breaks up the hard soil, the blade on the front of the bulldozer can push it away.

Scraping down

A bulldozer sometimes pulls a **scraper** behind it. This smaller machine scrapes the ground and carries away dirt. Then the bulldozer makes the ground smooth.

Bigger and faster

Most bulldozers have steel crawler tracks. The exception is the **High-Speed Dozer**, or HSD. Its tracks are rubber, allowing the speedy machine to travel up to 18 miles per hour (29 kph). That's 3 times as fast as a regular dozer! The rubber tracks also let the HSD ride over paved roads without doing any damage.

What else can a bulldozer do?

- This powerhouse of a machine can tear down small buildings.

- It is used in landscaping to clear trees and rubble.

- It can lift lumber and other building materials to move them from one place to another.

The excavator

An excavator's main job is digging. You could say that it works like a big shovel. A very big shovel!

The **boom**, the long part of the machine's **arm**, has a far reach and can swing from side to side.

Crawler tracks are giant steel belts that rotate, causing the machine to move forward or backward.

At the end of the arm is a **bucket** with sharp teeth for digging.

The **cab** sits on a platform that can turn all the way around.

Lowering (and raising) the boom

Like each of your arms, the boom has parts that bend, called **joints**. The boom comes down, and the bucket grabs dirt from the ground. Then it goes back up, lifting the dirt. The bucket opens and dumps its load onto the ground or into a dump truck.

Grapple hook

The **grapple hook** has four metal claws. Excavators use the hook to lift rubble, lumber, and other hard-to-grab things.

FUN FACT

An excavator can use different kinds of buckets. This one is called a **clamshell bucket** because it opens and closes like the shell of a clam.

Digging the foundation

One of the excavator's most important jobs on the construction site is digging the foundation for a house or building. Without a sturdy foundation, a building might **topple**, or fall over. An excavator digs deep to make sure this never happens.

From small to big

Excavators come in many sizes. The smaller ones dig holes only a few feet deep. The big excavators dig holes as deep as 45 feet (13.5 m), big enough to fit a house inside. Really big ones dig foundations for skyscrapers.

The smallest excavators are called **compact** or **mini-excavators**. They are used when work has to be done in small spaces. Some of these machines are small enough to fit through doorways.

Did You Know?

The taller the building, the deeper the foundation has to be. For tall buildings, long posts called **piles** are pounded into the ground. This is usually done with an excavator using an attachment called a **pile driver**. The piles are driven in until they hit very hard ground or rock, called **bedrock**. The piles can go down 100 feet (30.5 m) or more. When they're in place, they hold up the foundation.

The backhoe

A backhoe does two jobs. First, it digs up dirt. Then it turns around and picks up the loose dirt to load it into a dump truck. How does it do both things? It has an arm with a bucket for digging and a loader for lifting and carrying. Because it can do so much, sometimes a backhoe is the only big machine needed on a small job.

The **seat** swivels so the operator can work either the bucket or the loader.

The cab sits on top of the **carriage**.

The **loader** scoops up dirt and carries it away.

Backhoes have 2 sets of **wheels**. The big ones ride easily over rough land.

Stabilizer legs keep the backhoe steady.

The **boom** moves the arm and bucket from side to side.

This backhoe is lifting heavy cement using a grapple hook.

The long **arm** can reach out and dig down deep.

The **bucket** is used for digging.

Did You Know?

The backhoe's name is made up of 2 words: **back** and **hoe**. A hoe is a long-handled digging tool. On this mighty machine, the back bucket, or hoe, digs by dragging earth backward toward the machine.

Backhoe versus excavator

Sometimes it's hard to tell the difference between a backhoe and an excavator. They are both diggers, and they look alike, but they do different jobs.

What's the difference?

A backhoe digs like an excavator, but it also loads. It has a loader in front and a digger in back.

The bigger digger

Which is the bigger digger? An excavator is usually bigger. The largest John Deere excavator is 7 times bigger than the largest John Deere backhoe.

The operator of a backhoe has a hard job. To work the backhoe digger, he has to use the lever and drive the machine at the same time. And he also has to know how to work the loader. Plus, he always has to make sure there's enough room to swing the machine around. Operating this machine takes a lot of training, skill, and experience.

The loader

This big machine's main job is to load dirt and rubble into trucks. Besides lifting and carrying, a loader sometimes does other jobs, such as digging long, narrow ditches called **trenches**. True, it can't dig deep holes like an excavator or a backhoe. But those machines can't lift as well as a loader.

The operator uses a **joystick** to lift, tilt, and lower the bucket.

bucket

cab

Thick tires help support this heavy machine. In icy weather, the tires may be partly filled with water. This makes the tires heavier and the loader sturdier.

Articulated loaders, like this one, have a hinge that lets them bend in the middle. This makes driving around tight corners much easier.

The bucket can be replaced by other tools. This loader has a **forklift** with prongs that slide into wooden trays called **pallets**. The pallets can be stacked with wood, bricks, or cement blocks.

Most loaders have wheels, but some have crawler tracks like these. Wheels make the machine go faster, but crawler tracks grip the ground better.

The skid steer

A skid steer is like a loader, but it's smaller. A skid steer can turn more easily than bigger machines. This small machine is a big help on the construction site. It's good at lifting, like a loader, and it can fit into small spaces. Because a skid steer's arms are so close to its body, it can lift much higher than a loader.

The **engine** is in the back.

Two arms run alongside the cab.

The **loader** carries the dirt.

The wheels can **pivot**, or turn in a circle.

A skid steer can use up to 100 attachments. Here are just a few.

hammer

forklift

roller

broom

trencher

The dump truck

On the construction site, a dump truck is used to carry sand, gravel, dirt, or other loose material. It can take whatever it's carrying from one place on the site to another. Or it can carry its load to a different site, such as a dump. When it's time to unload, the operator unhooks the gate in back. Then he moves a lever inside the cab that tips the dump box.

The **gate** opens to dump out dirt.

The **dump box** is where the dirt is carried.

Dump trucks can have 6 or 8 wheels.

Big loads

A dump truck is a big, strong machine. A medium-sized dump truck can hold more than 13 tons of gravel. That's the weight of 3 large elephants. Some extra-large dump trucks can hold more than 500 tons.

Did You Know?

Some dump trucks have a hinge that connects the front cab and back bed. This lets the dump trucks make sharp turns.

Teamwork

No one construction machine can do everything. Each one has its own special purpose, and the machines work as a team to get the job done.

A dump truck's best friend

The dump truck often teams up with the excavator, the backhoe, or the loader.

- First, the machine that is digging scoops up the soil and rubble and puts it into the dump box.

- Then the dump truck carries the load away and dumps it.

Teamwork on the road

Wherever you see a road being built, you'll see teamwork in action. The bulldozer levels the ground and pushes the dirt and rubble into a pile. Then an excavator or backhoe picks it up and puts it into the dump truck.

What happens to all the dirt?

Where does all that dirt go after the excavator and other machines dig it up?

- Some is used to fill holes on the same site in another place.

- Some is stored to use on another job.

- Some is sold to other builders for use on other construction sites.

Jobs on the construction site

Most buildings are put together by a team of people.
On big projects, such as tall buildings or amusement parks,
there are many kinds of workers on the construction site.

An **architect** designs the building.
He thinks about how the building
will be used and how it will look.
He draws plans and makes
models to show to the
building's owner.

A **plumber** puts in pipes for water and checks that the bathtubs, toilets, and sinks work properly.

An **electrical engineer** makes sure that all the things that use electricity will work properly.

A **general contractor** hires the other workers and orders the machines and building materials.

A **mechanical engineer** plans the heating and cooling.

A **foreman** is the boss of the workers on the job.

A **welder** joins pieces of metal using heat.

Becoming a construction worker

Would you like to run one of the big machines? Or maybe you want to become one of the other workers on the construction site. Here's what you have to do.

Construction machines look fun to operate, but it takes a lot of skill. Many machine operators go to special schools to learn how to do this. Some learn from operators on the site.

Architects and engineers study for many years to learn how to design a building. They have to pass special tests before they can work on a building project.

On many sites, you need a high school diploma to be a helper. Some workers start as helpers and learn to do other jobs on the site, such as **carpentry**, or wood building.

Apprentices learn from skilled workers, such as machine operators, plumbers, electricians, or welders. Apprentices often go to a **trade school** to learn about electricity, plumbing, and other trades. A **trade** is a job that requires a certain set of skills. Apprentice programs are offered at construction companies and on construction sites, too.

What's on the site?

Here are some of the things you'll find on a construction site besides the big machines.

Trailers

The number of trailers on a site depends on the size of the job. There is usually a trailer used as a **jobsite office** for the foreman or the contractor. The jobsite office is where the contractor and the architect keep track of what's going on. It's also a place to post notices and important information.

Trailer uses

There can also be separate trailers for all the different kinds of work. Sometimes the electricians, plumbers, and carpenters have their own separate trailers. On a big site, the architects and engineers have their own trailers, too.

There's also a **toilet trailer** for the workers to use.

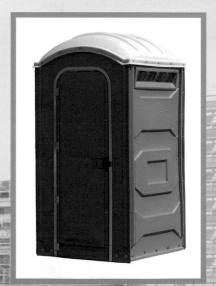

Storage containers

Both large and small **storage containers** hold supplies and tools. On big sites, you might find containers for electrical supplies, plumbing supplies, carpenters' tools, and more.

Soil and rubble are loaded into **Dumpsters** until they're carted away.

Building materials

If you look around the construction site, you'll see all kinds of building materials.

Wood beams

Lumber is wood that has been cut into long planks to be used for building. Some smaller pieces of wood are called **two-by-fours** because they are 2 inches (5 cm) thick and 4 inches (10 cm) wide. They can be cut into many lengths, from a few feet up to 24 feet (7.3 m) long.

Steel beams

Steel is a strong building metal made mostly from iron ore. The ore is mixed with other minerals and heated in a large furnace until it turns into a liquid. It's then shaped into beams. After they have cooled, the beams are hard and very strong.

Nails, screws, and **bolts** are usually made from steel, too. Some are made from **stainless steel,** a special kind of steel that doesn't rust.

Sheets of glass

Most glass is hard but **brittle.** It can crack or shatter easily. It is used for windows and sometimes for doors. The glass used in building construction is made in a special way so that it won't shatter and fall to the ground.

Slabs of marble

Marble is a hard rock that can be polished until it's very shiny.

Granite is a rock like marble, but it's even harder. Both marble and granite are used in many ways, such as on countertops, floors, and walls.

WHERE DOES IT COME FROM?

Lumber: We get wood from forests all over the world. In the United States, a lot of lumber comes from the Northwest, from states like Washington and Oregon.

Steel: The iron ore in steel is mined from the earth. The countries that mine the most iron ore are China and Brazil.

Marble and granite: These rocks come from **quarries**, deep pits in the earth. In the United States, most marble and granite come from Maine, Vermont, and Missouri. Some people think that the most beautiful marble comes from Italy.

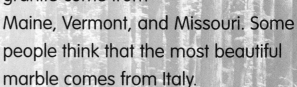

Building blocks

Besides beams of wood and steel, cement blocks are a basic building material.

Bricks are made from **clay** that has been hardened by heat. Clay is made out of minerals. It is sticky when wet but hard when dry.

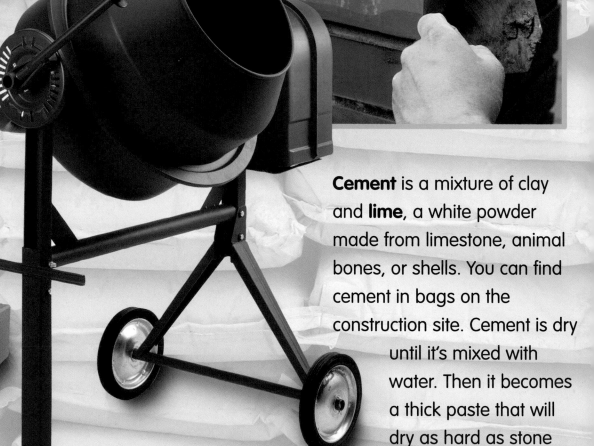

Cement is a mixture of clay and **lime**, a white powder made from limestone, animal bones, or shells. You can find cement in bags on the construction site. Cement is dry until it's mixed with water. Then it becomes a thick paste that will dry as hard as stone over time.

Concrete is formed when cement is mixed with water, sand, and broken stone or gravel. Then it is made into hard **concrete blocks**.

Cinder blocks are also made of cement. Added to the cement are little bits of **cinders**, which are tiny pieces of burned coal or wood. Cinder blocks are usually 8 inches by 12 inches by 18 inches (20 cm by 30 cm by 46 cm). Because they are strong, they're used for foundations in some houses and for walls in big buildings.

Did You Know?

The sand, clay, and pebbles in cement, concrete, and bricks come from riverbeds, beaches, and deserts all over the world.

Tools

Big machines do lots of jobs on the construction site. But for some jobs, the work has to be done with smaller tools, either hand tools or power tools.

Hand tools

A **hammer** drives in nails or pulls them out.

A **sledgehammer** has a large, heavy, flat head attached to a handle. Sledgehammers are often used in construction work for breaking through walls.

A **saw** cuts wood.

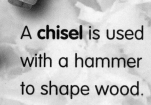

A **chisel** is used with a hammer to shape wood.

In the box

On a construction site, hand tools are kept in a **toolbox**. It's sometimes called a company toolbox or gang box.

Power tools

A **jackhammer** works like both a hammer and chisel in one. It's usually used to break up rock and pavement.

Power saws cut through wood faster than handsaws.

Nail guns shoot nails into wood.

A **tamper** pushes down soil to make it hard.

Power drills put in screws and drill holes.

Taking down buildings

Sometimes buildings have to be **demolished**, either by knocking them down or blowing them up. They might be crumbling or ready to fall down. Sometimes old buildings are demolished to make way for new buildings.

Big hammers

Backhoes and excavators with hammer attachments are used to smash into walls and break up paved streets and roads.

Bring in the big machines

A very small building, like a shed, can be demolished quickly and easily using a sledgehammer. Houses and other midsized buildings can be demolished using sledgehammers and jackhammers. Big buildings are usually demolished by big machines.

Explosions

Very large buildings and other structures, such as bridges, are sometimes demolished using **explosives**. **Dynamite** is a very powerful explosive that is used in the demolition of buildings.

Implosions

If a building is near other buildings, an explosion could damage those buildings. So, the building is **imploded**. Instead of everything flying outward, the building implodes, or collapses inward. This is done by carefully setting up the explosions to go off in sections. Each section of the building is designed to fall toward the center.

Safety on the site

A construction site is a busy—and dangerous—place. Big machines are at work. Heavy loads of lumber and steel are raised high off the ground. Powerful tools are often in use. That's why it's important to put safety first.

Keep away!

Safety cones and yellow tape mark off areas that nonworkers are not allowed to enter.

UNDER CONSTRUCTION

SAFETY FOOTWEAR MUST BE WORN IN THIS AREA

DANGER HARD HAT AREA

AUTHORIZED PERSONNEL ONLY HARD HATS REQUIRED

NOTICE SAFETY GLASSES MUST BE WORN

Did You Know?

All big machines make beeping noises when they back up. That's because the operator can't always see what's in back of the machine. The beeping warns the other workers that the machine is coming.

Safety signs

Safety signs at construction sites and near roadwork tell workers and visitors how to be careful and stay safe.

Safety netting

Netting made of nylon is often used to cover parts of a building while construction is under way. The netting keeps falling pieces of stone or brick from hitting people below.

Bad weather conditions

The best time for building is when the weather is mild and sunny. It's hard for construction workers to stay outdoors for long periods of time in the cold. It can also be dangerous because of ice, which is very slippery. When it rains, the ground is also slippery, and it's hard for workers to see what they're doing.

Sometimes, when the weather turns really bad, the work has to stop. The machines can't do their jobs very well, and it's hard to clear the land or dig a foundation in rain or snow. Work also stops on tall buildings when the wind is strong, because of the danger of falling objects.

Construction gear

Construction workers use all kinds of gear to keep themselves safe.

A **hard hat** protects a worker's head from falling rocks and other debris.

Workers wear **ear protectors** to muffle loud noises.

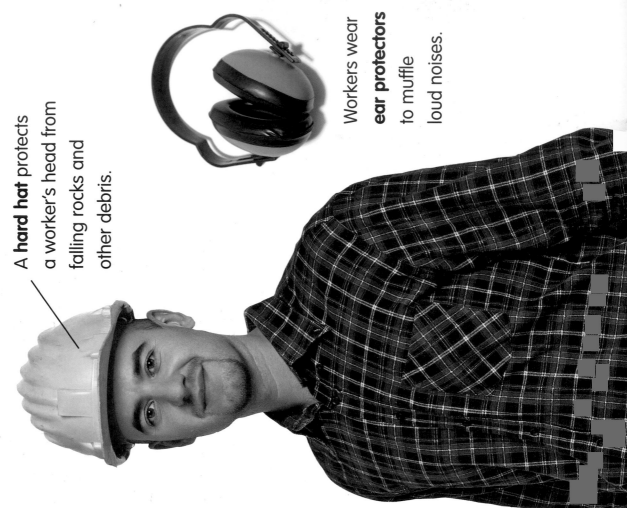

A **bright-colored vest** is easily spotted by other workers. Sometimes the vests have tape that reflects light so that they stand out even more.

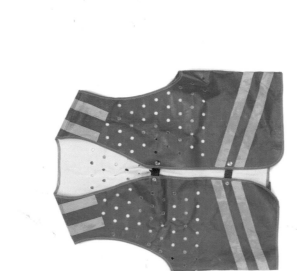

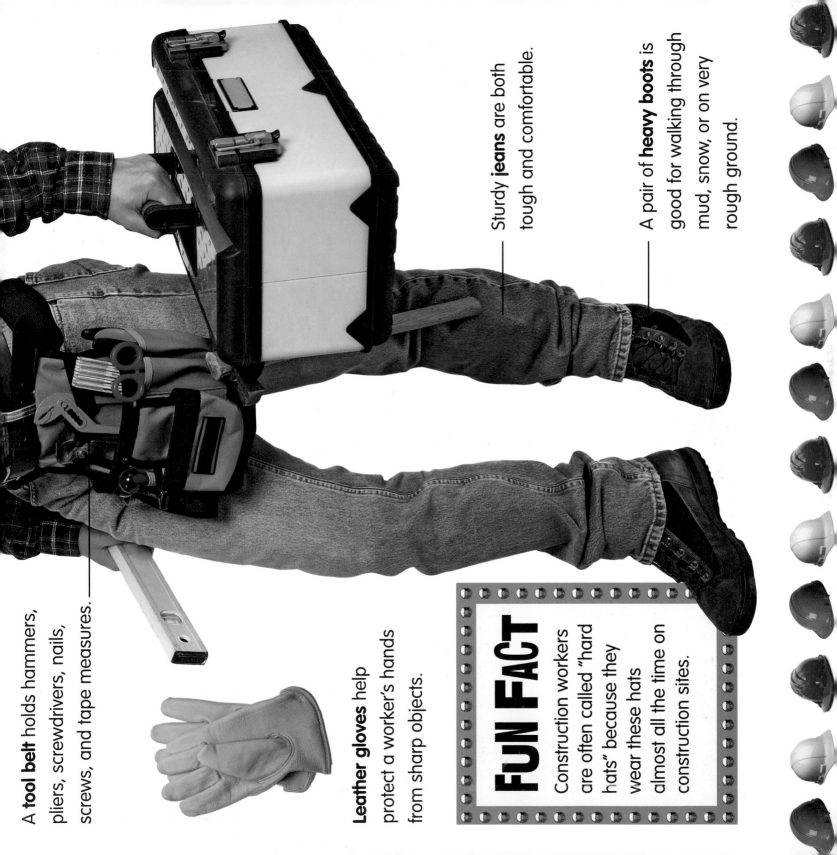

Sturdy **jeans** are both tough and comfortable.

A pair of **heavy boots** is good for walking through mud, snow, or on very rough ground.

A **tool belt** holds hammers, pliers, screwdrivers, nails, screws, and tape measures.

Leather gloves help protect a worker's hands from sharp objects.

FUN FACT

Construction workers are often called "hard hats" because they wear these hats almost all the time on construction sites.

Building long ago

Building today is very different than it was three, two, or even one hundred years ago. Before construction machines were invented, all buildings were built by hand. Here's a look at ways we built in the past.

Early buildings were made with handheld tools like these.

Until about one hundred years ago, horses and oxen were used to pull carts and wagons filled with bricks, lumber, bags of cement, and other materials for building.

There were no machines for building until the first successful steam engine was invented in 1712. Steam was then used to power excavators, bulldozers, and steamrollers for many years.

Horsepower

Before engines were invented, teams of horses were used for heavy work, such as pulling wagons. James Watt, a Scottish engineer and inventor who improved on the design of the steam engine, figured out how much work a horse could do per minute. He called this **horsepower**. A bulldozer today can have a 500-horsepower engine. That means that it would take about 500 horses to do the work of one bulldozer.

The grader

Big machines don't just work on buildings. Some of them, like the grader, work on roads. A grader has a long **blade** that levels, or smooths out, dirt. Once the ground has been prepared, **asphalt** can be put down to make a paved road. Asphalt is a mixture of **pitch** and **gravel** or sand. Pitch is usually made from oil. Gravel is made out of pounded stones.

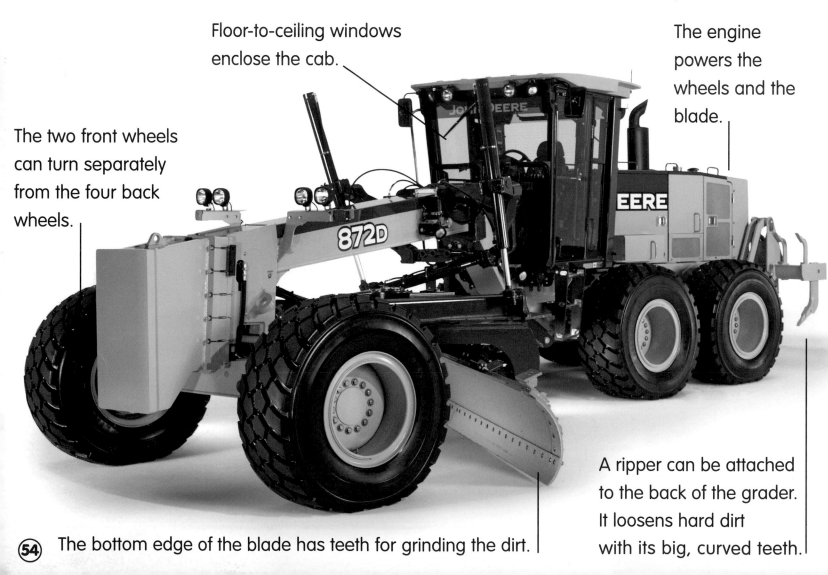

Floor-to-ceiling windows enclose the cab.

The engine powers the wheels and the blade.

The two front wheels can turn separately from the four back wheels.

A ripper can be attached to the back of the grader. It loosens hard dirt with its big, curved teeth.

The bottom edge of the blade has teeth for grinding the dirt.

Finishing touches

Besides taking care of roads, graders are used on construction sites for other jobs. After an old building is torn down, they clean up the site and make the ground smooth. Graders can also dig shallow holes or smooth out the ground before pavement is put in.

Snow day

In winter, the grader has another job. It works as a snowplow, clearing snow from the road with an angled blade called a **wing blade**. The grader pushes the snow to one side of the road.

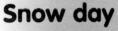

How a road is built

Just like a building, a road must be planned. Where will it go? How wide will it be? What will it be made of? Only when the plan is finished can the roadwork begin.

Tearing things down

Sometimes, before a road can be built, buildings or trees have to be removed. Big machines, like this excavator, are used for the job. Bulldozers and cranes can be used, too.

Smoothing out the ground

Big machines are brought in to smooth out the ground.

First, a bulldozer pushes dirt and rubble aside.

Next, a scraper goes over the cleared ground to remove any remaining bumps.

Finally, a grader smooths out the ground.

Paving the road

A paved road is made of layers of stones. The biggest stones are on the bottom, and the smallest ones are on the top. Asphalt is put down last.

A steamroller presses down the stones. That forms the **roadbed**, or foundation.

Next, a dump truck backs up to a machine called a **paver**.

The dump truck dumps the hot asphalt into a **hopper**, a storage container in the paver.

The paver moves slowly to spread the asphalt on the roadbed.

Did You Know?

The foundation for a road has to be built higher than the land around it. That way, rainwater can drain off the road, and roadways won't flood.

Construction sites at night

Shh! The machines are sleeping!
Most of the time, construction work shuts down at night. The workers go home, and the machines are silent. A night watchman guards the site, making sure that no one takes any tools or touches the machines. In the morning, work will begin again.

Working at night

Sometimes work goes on at night because a job has to be done in a hurry. That's called a **rush job**. Floodlights shine brightly to help the workers see. The workers also use flashlights for close-up work.

Safety at night

When a night job is under way, it's especially important to keep everyone safe. All workers wear bright yellow or orange vests. On many sites, they wear reflective clothing so they can be seen from a long way off. Because it's hard for machine operators to see behind them in the dark, workers listen for the beeping sounds the machines make when they back up.

The big machines off-site

Before they can do their work, big machines have to get to the jobsite. Most of them are sent in trailers. Sometimes they're put on large flatbed trucks. A few of the wheeled machines get to the site on their own. Big machines that use crawler tracks are not permitted on roads because the tracks might damage the surface.

Did You Know?

Any big machine that travels on public roads must have a sign that says SLOW MOVING VEHICLE to alert other drivers.

Where do the big machines "sleep" at night?

At night, the machines usually stay on the construction site until the job is done. In cities, they may be loaded onto flatbed trucks and taken to special parking areas at the end of the day.

On the sidelines

When a job is completed, the machines go back to the construction companies. They're stored in big yards until it's time to work on the next job. Between jobs, they are inspected and repaired, repainted, and kept in good working condition.

Completed building

When the construction is done, a brand-new building stands where the construction site used to be. Soon, people will come to work or live in the building. Before that happens, some finishing touches remain.

A **building inspector** looks at a building many times as it is being built. When a building is finished, it gets a final inspection. Once the building passes inspection, people can start using it.

A **custodian** for the new building is hired. The custodian and his staff will keep the building clean and make repairs.

The architects and engineers stop by to look at the building they designed. They take notes of things they've learned to use on future projects.

A **landscaper** plants trees and shrubs and waters flowers.

Photo credits

The publisher would like to thank the following for their kind permission to reproduce their photographs:

ABBREVIATIONS KEY: t-top, b-bottom, r-right, l-left, c-center, a-above, f-far, bkgd-background, bo-border

Cover Images
Front Jason Vandehey/Shutterstock.com (tr)
Back Morgan Lane Photography/Shutterstock.com (cr)
8-9 Elen-a Elisseeva/Shutterstock.com (8l); Tish1/Shutterstock.com (8r); Cynthia Farmer/Shutterstock.com (9tl); Pres Panayotov/Shutterstock.com (9bl); luchschen/Shutterstock.com (9tr); Losevsky Pavel/Shutterstock.com (9br)
10-11 Lisa F. Young/Shutterstock.com (10l); David Lee/Shutterstock.com (11bl); Stephen Coburn/Shutterstock.com (11r)
30-31 astroskeptic/Shutterstock.com (bo)
34-35 Lisa F. Young/Shutterstock.com (34tr); Rob Marmion/Shutterstock.com (34cr); Lisa F. Young/Shutterstock.com (34br); Steve Lovegrove/Shutterstock.com (34tl); Joe Gough/Shutterstock.com (34cl); Kevin Penhallow/Shutterstock.com (34bl); James Steidl/Shutterstock.com (35)
36-37 Chad McDermott/Shutterstock.com (37tl); Lisa F. Young/Shutterstock.com (37bl); Shootov Igor/Shutterstock.com (37tr)
38-39 Tatjana Strelkova/Shutterstock.com (bkgd); travis manley/Shutterstock.com (38l); WilleeCole/Shutterstock.com (38r); Nicholas Moore/Shutterstock.com (39t); 1125089601/Shutterstock.com (39b)
40-41 STILLFX/Shutterstock.com (40bkgd); zeber/Shutterstock.com (41bkgd); Marek Pawluczuk/Shutterstock.com (40t); Dwight Smith/Shutterstock.com (40b); Aleksey Kondratyuk/Shutterstock.com (41tl); mrfotos/Shutterstock.com (41bl); jason scott duggan/Shutterstock.com (41tr); José Correia Marafona/Shutterstock.com (41br)
42-43 Shi Yali/Shutterstock.com (bkgd); jeff gynane/Shutterstock.com (bo); Robert Redelowski/Shutterstock.com (42bl); William Milner/Shutterstock.com (42c); Dima Kalinin/Shutterstock.com (42tr); Lagui/Shutterstock.com (43)
44-45 Natalia Yudenich/Shutterstock.com (bkgd); STILLFX/Shutterstock.com (bo); STILLFX/Shutterstock.com (44tl); Tischenko Irina/Shutterstock.com (44bl); kozvic49/Shutterstock.com (44tr); Ruslan Kokarev/Shutterstock.com (44bc); Infomages/Shutterstock.com (44br); Margie Hurwich/Shutterstock.com (45tl); microstocker/Shutterstock.com (45tc); Yegor Korzh/Shutterstock.com (45br); Roger Dale Pleis/Shutterstock.com (45bl); 7505811966/Shutterstock.com (45tr)
46-47 stocksnapp/Shutterstock.com (bkgd); Leonid Shcheglov/Shutterstock.com (46t); Doug Stevens/Shutterstock.com (46b)
48-49 Julián Rovagnati/Shutterstock.com (48bkgd); Robert J. Beyers II/Shutterstock.com (rtl); max blain/Shutterstock.com (rtc); Andreas Gradin/Shutterstock.com (rtr); David Dea/Shutterstock.com (rbl); Stephen Finn/Shutterstock.com (rbc); Kris Butler/Shutterstock.com (rbr); Seleznev Oleg/Shutterstock.com (49bkgd); Cecilia Lim H M/Shutterstock.com (49l)
50-51 Alberto Pérez Veiga/Shutterstock.com (bo); Morgan Lane Photography/Shutterstock.com (bo); J. Helgason/Shutterstock.com (bo); ZanyZeus/Shutterstock.com (50tr); R/Shutterstock.com (51tr); STILLFX/Shutterstock.com (51br); altiso/Shutterstock.com (50-51c);
52-53 Lukiyanova Natalia/Shutterstock.com (bo); Dario Sabljak/Shutterstock.com (52l); Donald R. Swartz/Shutterstock.com (53tr)
58-59 Artur Bogacki/Shutterstock.com (58bkgd); Chin Kok Wei/Shutterstock.com (59l)
62-63 Lisa F. Young/Shutterstock.com (62l); CHRISTOPHE ROLLAND/Shutterstock.com (62r); Neo Edmund/Shutterstock.com (63tl); Teresa Azevedo/Shutterstock.com (63tc); Lisa F. Young/Shutterstock.com (63bl); V. J. Matthew/Shutterstock.com (63cr); Christina Richards/Shutterstock.com (63br)
Endpapers Tatjana Strelkova/Shutterstock.com

All other images © Deere & Company.

Every effort has been made to trace the copyright holders of photographs, and we apologize if any omissions have been made.